RACHEL WOJO

Pure Joy

cultivating a
happy heart

BIBLE READING PLAN & JOURNAL

PURE JOY
Bible Reading Plan and Journal
PUBLISHED BY RACHEL WOJO
Copyright © 2016 by Rachel Wojnarowski
This title is also available as an eBook for Kindle
Visit **www.rachelwojo.com/shop**

Requests for information should be addressed to rachel@rachelwojo.com

Trade Paperback ISBN 978-1540896018
eBook ISBN 1540896013

Cover design by Rachel Wojnarowski

Library of Congress Cataloging-in-Publication Data

Printed in the United States of America
2016—First Edition

Table of Contents

	Intro: Cultivating a Happy Heart
	A Personal Note from Rachel
Day 1	Psalm 47:1-9
Day 2	1 Peter 1:3-9
Day 3	Romans 15:7-13
Day 4	Nehemiah 8:5-10
Day 5	John 16:17-24
Day 6	Psalm 30:1-5
Day 7	Hebrews 12:1-6
Day 8	Psalm 4:1-8
Day 9	Eccles. 5:12-20
Day 10	Isaiah 35:4-10
Day 11	Jeremiah 15:10-16
Day 12	Matthew 2:1-10
Day 13	Psalm 51:7-12
Day 14	Psalm 65:1-13
Day 15	Habakkuk 3:12-19

Table of Contents

Day 16   John 15:5-11

Day 17   Galatians 5:22-26

Day 18   Psalm 92:1-8

Day 19   Philippians 2:1-11

Day 20   1 Thess. 1:4-10

Day 21   James 1:1-6

Day 22   Jude 1:20-25

Day 23   Psalm 84:1-7

Day 24   Psalm 97:1-12

Day 25   Eccles. 2:22-26

Day 26   Isaiah 29:13-19

Day 27   Isaiah 35:1-10

Day 28   Psalm 119:105-112

Day 29   Eccles. 8:12-17

Day 30   Psalm 126:1-6

Day 31   Isaiah 9:1-7

A Personal Note from Rachel

Dear Friend,

Thank you for joining this joy journey with me. My goal through Bible reading is to draw closer to Jesus, and I want that for you too!

Through reading daily Bible passages, praying, and listening to God, we're going to nurture and grow our relationship with him. This Bible reading plan and journal is specifically focused on true joy. The kind with which a simple feel-good song can't compete. The kind that lingers when times are hard. The kind of joy that can only come from above.

I.can't.wait!

Rachel

Cultivating a Happy Heart

Welcome to the Pure Joy Journal. I'm so excited to start this journey with you. For the next thirty-one days, we are going to dig into God's word and grow closer to Him. Together we'll make the choice to cultivate a happy heart by reading God's Word and applying it in our daily lives.

> Joy has nothing to do with religion. Relationship with the heavenly Father, not religion, results in joy. Religion offers lists; relationships offer love. I've found that many people practice religion and fewer people promote relationship. Joy is a natural result of fostering a relationship with God.
> – *One More Step*

You can share what you are learning on social media by using the hashtags #purejoy and #biblereading or you can just keep it between you and God.

Are you ready to get started?

Step 1:

Pray: Spend some time with God in prayer. Prayer is simply having a conversation with him.

Step 2:

Read the Bible passage for the day one time slowly, soaking in each phrase. Read again if time allows.

Step 3:

Complete the JOY journal prompts reflecting on your current situation or circumstances.

Step 4:

Think over your plan for the day and answer the daily question.

Jesus

I'm thankful for Jesus because:

_____

_____

_____

Others

I'm thankful for: _____

because of _____

_____

_____

Yourself

I'm thankful for this personal blessing:

_____

_____

_____

Praise

Praising the Lord demolishes discouragement.

What will I do today to live joyfully because I know joy lives in me? How can I put my thanks into action?

_____

_____

_____

_____

_____

_____

_____

_____

Pen A Prayer

_____

_____

_____

_____

_____

_____

_____

_____

Jesus

I'm thankful for Jesus because:

_____

_____

_____

Others

I'm thankful for: _____

because of _____

_____

_____

Rejoice

Christ's resurrection provides a reason for rejoicing.

Yourself

I'm thankful for this personal blessing:

_____

_____

_____

What will I do today to live joyfully because I know joy lives in me? How can I put my thanks into action?

_____
_____
_____
_____
_____
_____
_____
_____

Pen A Prayer

_____
_____
_____
_____
_____
_____
_____
_____

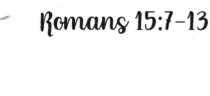

Jesus

I'm thankful for Jesus because:

_____

_____

_____

Others

I'm thankful for: _____

because of _____

_____

_____

Yourself

I'm thankful for this personal blessing:

_____

_____

_____

Peace

Believing in the God of hope brings joy and peace.

What will I do today to live joyfully because I know joy lives in me? How can I put my thanks into action?

_____

_____

_____

_____

_____

_____

_____

_____

_____

Pen A Prayer

_____

_____

_____

_____

_____

_____

_____

_____

_____

Jesus

I'm thankful for Jesus because:

_____

_____

_____

Others

I'm thankful for: _____

because of _____

_____

_____

Strength

The choice to keep going usually begins with the choice to adopt joy.

Yourself

I'm thankful for this personal blessing:

_____

_____

_____

What will I do today to live joyfully because I know joy lives in me? How can I put my thanks into action?

_____
_____
_____
_____
_____
_____
_____
_____

Pen A Prayer

_____
_____
_____
_____
_____
_____
_____
_____

Jesus

I'm thankful for Jesus because:

_____

_____

_____

Promise

I can
rejoice for
the promise of
His coming.

Others

I'm thankful for: _____

because of _____

_____

_____

Yourself

I'm thankful for this personal blessing:

_____

_____

_____

What will I do today to live joyfully because I know joy lives in me? How can I put my thanks into action?

_____
_____
_____
_____
_____
_____
_____
_____

Pen A Prayer

_____
_____
_____
_____
_____
_____
_____
_____
_____

Jesus

I'm thankful for Jesus because:

_____

_____

_____

Others

I'm thankful for:

_____

because of _____

_____

_____

Yourself

I'm thankful for this personal blessing:

_____

_____

_____

Restored

My God brought me from the pit and for this I can rejoice!

What will I do today to live joyfully because I know joy lives in me? How can I put my thanks into action?

_____
_____
_____
_____
_____
_____
_____
_____

Pen A Prayer

_____
_____
_____
_____
_____
_____
_____
_____

Whether you stand
high on the
mountaintop
or low in the valley,
let the joy of Jesus
flood your soul in
praise for who he is-
the God of the
universe
and your best
friend.

Jesus

I'm thankful for Jesus because:

_____

_____

_____

Others

I'm thankful for: _____

because of _____

_____

_____

Yourself

I'm thankful for this personal blessing:

_____

_____

_____

Endurance

For the joy
set before
Him, Christ
endured.

What will I do today to live joyfully because I know joy lives in me? How can I put my thanks into action?

_____
_____
_____
_____
_____
_____
_____
_____

Pen A Prayer

_____
_____
_____
_____
_____
_____
_____
_____
_____

Psalm 4:1-8

Jesus

I'm thankful for Jesus because:

_____
_____
_____

Others

I'm thankful for: _____
because of _____
_____
_____

Yourself

I'm thankful for this personal blessing:

_____
_____
_____

Greater Joy

Nothing in this world brings joy like that of knowing Jesus.

What will I do today to live joyfully because I know joy lives in me? How can I put my thanks into action?

_____
_____
_____
_____
_____
_____
_____
_____
_____

Pen A Prayer

_____
_____
_____
_____
_____
_____
_____
_____
_____

Ecclesiastes 5:12-20

Jesus

I'm thankful for Jesus because:

_____

_____

_____

Occupied

God keeps
me occupied
with joy in my
heart.

Others

I'm thankful for: _____

because of _____

_____

_____

Yourself

I'm thankful for this personal blessing:

_____

_____

_____

What will I do today to live joyfully because I know joy lives in me? How can I put my thanks into action?

_____
_____
_____
_____
_____
_____
_____
_____

Pen A Prayer

_____
_____
_____
_____
_____
_____
_____
_____

Jesus

I'm thankful for Jesus because:

_____
_____
_____

 **Redeemed**

Others

Sorrow and
sighing
shall flee
away.

I'm thankful for: _____
because of _____
_____
_____

Yourself

I'm thankful for this personal blessing:

_____
_____
_____

What will I do today to live joyfully because I know joy lives in me? How can I put my thanks into action?

_____
_____
_____
_____
_____
_____
_____
_____

Pen A Prayer

_____
_____
_____
_____
_____
_____
_____
_____

Jesus

I'm thankful for Jesus because:

_____

_____

_____

Others

I'm thankful for: _____

because of _____

_____

_____

Yourself

I'm thankful for this personal blessing:

_____

_____

_____

Delight

Is God's
Word the
delight of
my heart?

What will I do today to live joyfully because I know joy lives in me? How can I put my thanks into action?

_____
_____
_____
_____
_____
_____
_____
_____

Pen A Prayer

_____
_____
_____
_____
_____
_____
_____
_____

I'm thankful for Jesus because:

_____

_____

_____

I'm thankful for: _____

because of _____

_____

_____

Presence

Rejoicing is present when I recognize he is near.

I'm thankful for this personal blessing:

_____

_____

_____

What will I do today to live joyfully because I know joy
lives in me? How can I put my thanks into action?

_____
_____
_____
_____
_____
_____
_____
_____

Pen A Prayer

_____
_____
_____
_____
_____
_____
_____
_____

Jesus

I'm thankful for Jesus because:

_____
_____
_____

Return

His joy is
available
again and
again.

Others

I'm thankful for: _____
because of _____
_____
_____

Yourself

I'm thankful for this personal blessing:

_____
_____
_____

What will I do today to live joyfully because I know joy lives in me? How can I put my thanks into action?

_____
_____
_____
_____
_____
_____
_____
_____

Pen A Prayer

_____
_____
_____
_____
_____
_____
_____
_____

God woke up half
the world this
morning with the
sun
as the other half he
tucked in with the
moon.
All the while he
orchestrated the
universe,
he whispered to
your soul: "Enjoy
the gift of another
day.
Another breath.
My joy."

Jesus

I'm thankful for Jesus because:

_____

_____

_____

Breathe

Enjoy the
gift of
another
day.

Others

I'm thankful for: _____

because of _____

_____

_____

Yourself

I'm thankful for this personal blessing:

_____

_____

_____

What will I do today to live joyfully because I know joy lives in me? How can I put my thanks into action?

_____

_____

_____

_____

_____

_____

_____

_____

Pen A Prayer

_____

_____

_____

_____

_____

_____

_____

_____

_____

Jesus

I'm thankful for Jesus because:

_____
_____
_____

Salvation

Take joy
in the
God of
salvation.

Others

I'm thankful for: _____

because of _____

_____

_____

Yourself

I'm thankful for this personal blessing:

_____
_____
_____

What will I do today to live joyfully because I know joy lives in me? How can I put my thanks into action?

_____

_____

_____

_____

_____

_____

_____

_____

Pen A Prayer

_____

_____

_____

_____

_____

_____

_____

_____

Jesus

I'm thankful for Jesus because:

_____
_____
_____

Others

I'm thankful for: _____
because of _____
_____
_____

Yourself

I'm thankful for this personal blessing:

_____
_____
_____

Abide

Joy is a result of living in relationship with Jesus.

What will I do today to live joyfully because I know joy
lives in me? How can I put my thanks into action?

_____

_____

_____

_____

_____

_____

_____

_____

Pen A Prayer

_____

_____

_____

_____

_____

_____

_____

_____

Jesus

I'm thankful for Jesus because:

_____

_____

_____

Others

I'm thankful for: _____

because of _____

_____

_____

Yourself

I'm thankful for this personal blessing:

_____

_____

_____

Fruit

When I walk in the Spirit, joy floods my soul.

What will I do today to live joyfully because I know joy lives in me? How can I put my thanks into action?

_____
_____
_____
_____
_____
_____
_____
_____
_____

Pen A Prayer

_____
_____
_____
_____
_____
_____
_____
_____
_____

Jesus

I'm thankful for Jesus because:

_____
_____
_____

Others

I'm thankful for: _____
because of _____
_____
_____

Yourself

I'm thankful for this personal blessing:

_____
_____
_____

Glad

The One who holds the sea in place, holds my heart.

What will I do today to live joyfully because I know joy lives in me? How can I put my thanks into action?

_____

_____

_____

_____

_____

_____

_____

_____

Pen A Prayer

_____

_____

_____

_____

_____

_____

_____

_____

Jesus

I'm thankful for Jesus because:

_____
_____
_____

Others

I'm thankful for: _____
because of _____
_____
_____

Yourself

I'm thankful for this personal blessing:

_____
_____
_____

Unity

Disunity
steals
my
joy.

What will I do today to live joyfully because I know joy lives in me? How can I put my thanks into action?

_____
_____
_____
_____
_____
_____
_____
_____

Pen A Prayer

_____
_____
_____
_____
_____
_____
_____
_____

Jesus

I'm thankful for Jesus because:

_____

_____

_____

Others

I'm thankful for: _____

because of _____

_____

_____

Yourself

I'm thankful for this personal blessing:

_____

_____

_____

Receive

The Word and the Spirit bring joy even in the midst of heartache.

What will I do today to live joyfully because I know joy lives in me? How can I put my thanks into action?

_____

_____

_____

_____

_____

_____

_____

_____

_____

Pen A Prayer

_____

_____

_____

_____

_____

_____

_____

_____

Encouragement
comes from Christ.
Love brings
comfort.
Sympathy stems
from the
Holy Spirit.
Unity brings joy.

esus

I'm thankful for Jesus because:

_____

_____

_____

Steadfast

Count trials joy because perseverance and faithfulness are developing.

 thers

I'm thankful for: _____

because of _____

_____

_____

 ourself

I'm thankful for this personal blessing:

_____

_____

_____

What will I do today to live joyfully because I know joy lives in me? How can I put my thanks into action?

_____

_____

_____

_____

_____

_____

_____

_____

Pen A Prayer

_____

_____

_____

_____

_____

_____

_____

Jesus

I'm thankful for Jesus because:

_____

_____

_____

Others

I'm thankful for: _____

because of _____

_____

_____

Yourself

I'm thankful for this personal blessing:

_____

_____

_____

Blameless

Christ presents
me to the throne
of God with
pure joy.

What will I do today to live joyfully because I know joy lives in me? How can I put my thanks into action?

_____

_____

_____

_____

_____

_____

_____

_____

Pen A Prayer

_____

_____

_____

_____

_____

_____

_____

_____

Jesus

I'm thankful for Jesus because:

_____
_____
_____

Sing

I serve
a living
God.

Others

I'm thankful for: _____
because of _____

_____
_____

Yourself

I'm thankful for this personal blessing:

_____
_____
_____

What will I do today to live joyfully because I know joy lives in me? How can I put my thanks into action?

_____
_____
_____
_____
_____
_____
_____
_____

Pen A Prayer

_____
_____
_____
_____
_____
_____
_____
_____

Jesus

I'm thankful for Jesus because:

_____
_____
_____

Others

I'm thankful for: _____
because of _____
_____
_____

Yourself

I'm thankful for this personal blessing:

_____
_____
_____

Be Glad

Light and joy walk hand in hand.

What will I do today to live joyfully because I know joy lives in me? How can I put my thanks into action?

_____

_____

_____

_____

_____

_____

_____

_____

Pen A Prayer

_____

_____

_____

_____

_____

_____

_____

_____

Jesus

I'm thankful for Jesus because:

_____
_____
_____

Others

I'm thankful for: _____
because of _____

_____
_____

Yourself

I'm thankful for this personal blessing:

_____
_____
_____

Gift

Joy is a gift from God.

What will I do today to live joyfully because I know joy lives in me? How can I put my thanks into action?

_____

_____

_____

_____

_____

_____

_____

_____

Pen A Prayer

_____

_____

_____

_____

_____

_____

_____

_____

Isaiah 29:13-19

Jesus

I'm thankful for Jesus because:

_____

_____

_____

Others

I'm thankful for: _____

because of _____

_____

_____

Yourself

I'm thankful for this personal blessing:

_____

_____

_____

Fresh

The Lord fills a
humble heart
anew.

What will I do today to live joyfully because I know joy
lives in me? How can I put my thanks into action?

_____
_____
_____
_____
_____
_____
_____
_____

Pen A Prayer

_____
_____
_____
_____
_____
_____
_____
_____

For every time the
thought crosses my
mind today that I'm
not good enough,
strong enough,
just "enough",
what if I replace it
with "Now to
him..."?
Because he presents
me before the
throne of God with
pure joy, as a
blameless daughter
of the King.

Jesus

I'm thankful for Jesus because:

_____

_____

_____

Others

I'm thankful for: _____

because of _____

_____

_____

Yourself

I'm thankful for this personal blessing:

_____

_____

_____

Restore

When I've lost my joy, the One who saved me offers healing.

What will I do today to live joyfully because I know joy lives in me? How can I put my thanks into action?

_____

_____

_____

_____

_____

_____

_____

_____

Pen A Prayer

_____

_____

_____

_____

_____

_____

_____

_____

Jesus

I'm thankful for Jesus because:

_____

_____

_____

Testimony

His word and His work bring joy.

Others

I'm thankful for: _____

because of _____

_____

_____

Yourself

I'm thankful for this personal blessing:

_____

_____

_____

What will I do today to live joyfully because I know joy lives in me? How can I put my thanks into action?

_____

_____

_____

_____

_____

_____

_____

_____

Pen A Prayer

_____

_____

_____

_____

_____

_____

_____

_____

Jesus

I'm thankful for Jesus because:

_____
_____
_____

Others

I'm thankful for: _____
because of _____
_____
_____

Yourself

I'm thankful for this personal blessing:

_____
_____
_____

Everlasting

I may not comprehend God's ways, but I can commend His joy.

What will I do today to live joyfully because I know joy lives in me? How can I put my thanks into action?

_____

_____

_____

_____

_____

_____

_____

_____

Pen A Prayer

_____

_____

_____

_____

_____

_____

_____

_____

Jesus

I'm thankful for Jesus because:

_____

_____

_____

Others

I'm thankful for: _____

because of _____

_____

_____

Yourself

I'm thankful for this personal blessing:

_____

_____

_____

Reflect

I can always look back on what God has done with joy.

What will I do today to live joyfully because I know joy lives in me? How can I put my thanks into action?

_____
_____
_____
_____
_____
_____
_____
_____

Pen A Prayer

_____
_____
_____
_____
_____
_____
_____
_____

Jesus

I'm thankful for Jesus because:

_____
_____
_____

Others

I'm thankful for: _____
because of _____
_____
_____

Yourself

I'm thankful for this personal blessing:

_____
_____
_____

Glad

The joy of Jesus
makes hearts
glad.

What will I do today to live joyfully because I know joy lives in me? How can I put my thanks into action?

_____

_____

_____

_____

_____

_____

_____

_____

Pen A Prayer

_____

_____

_____

_____

_____

_____

_____

_____

Put a Bow on It!

You did it! You read your Bible for 31 days in a row!

Discovering true joy in Jesus through reading his Word is such a gift. I pray that as you've walked this 31 day path, you've realized the wonder of beautiful joy.

Joy is not a one-time feeling; it's a lifetime choice.

Pure joy is rich and beautiful because Jesus brings us joy through saving and sustaining us. He is our joy.

Thanks for joining me on this journey through the Bible. Discover more Bible reading plans at rachelwojo.com/free-bible-printables/.

By his grace,
Rachel

About the Author

Rachel "Wojo" Wojnarowski is wife to Matt and mom to seven wonderful kids. Her greatest passion is inspiring others to welcome Jesus into their lives and enjoy the abundant life he offers.

As a sought-after blogger and writer, she sees thousands of readers visit her blog daily. Rachel leads community ladies' Bible studies in central Ohio and serves as an event planner and speaker. In her "free time" she crochets, knits, and sews handmade clothing. Okay, not really. She enjoys running and she's a tech geek at heart.

Reader, writer, speaker, and dreamer, Rachel can be found on her website at **www.RachelWojo.com.**

Free Bible Study Video Series

If you enjoyed this Bible reading plan & journal, then you'll love Rachel's free video Bible study to help you find strength for difficult seasons of life! **http://rachelwojo.com/free-bible-study-video-series-for-one-more-step/**

Feel like giving up?

Are you ready to quit? Give up? But deep down, you want to figure out how to keep on keeping on?

Like you, Rachel has faced experiences that crushed her dreams of the perfect life: a failed marriage, a daughter's heartbreaking diagnosis, and more. In this book, she transparently shares her pain and empathizes with yours, then points you to the path of God's Word, where you'll find hope to carry you forward. One More Step gives you permission to ache freely—and helps you believe that life won't always be this hard. No matter the circumstances you face, through these pages you'll learn to...

- persevere through out-of-control circumstances and gain a more intimate relationship with Jesus
- run to God's Word when discouragement strikes
- replace feelings of despair with truths of Scripture

BUY NOW
www.rachelwojo.com/onemorestep

If you enjoyed this Bible reading plan and journal, then you'll love:

http://rachelwojo.com/shop

Made in the USA
Lexington, KY
09 March 2018